Steck-Vaughn

Writer's Dictionary

Primary Level

This book belongs to:

Ellie Krantz

To the teacher: The *Steck-Vaughn Writer's Dictionary* is a spelling and vocabulary tool that can be used in a variety of ways. Students can use this dictionary to write words they misspell, words they want to remember, and words they have mastered. The pages for alphabetical entries are followed by pages for recording words in content areas such as social studies. Both kinds of pages provide space for writing words, pictorial and verbal definitions, and other information about words. The dictionary concludes with a list of words frequently misspelled by young children.

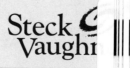

Steck
Vaughn

D1041819

www.Steck-Vaughn.c
1-800-531-5015

Aa

Boris the baby **anteater** said,

"**Apples** are my favorite treat."

"I like juicy apricots," said the **ape**.

The **alligator** just snarled "Meat!"

Aa

anteater

ape

apples

again   Australia

always

am

ant

are

awesome

acorn

aquamarine

A
B
C
D
E
F
G
H
I
J
K
L
M
N
O
P
Q
R
S
T
U
V
W
X
Y
Z

  alligator   ape   apples

A a

alligator

anteater

ape

Bb

When Benny looked in his **backpack**,

He found Bingo the **bat,**

A **bug** with spots all over,

Some **beans,** and Ringo the rat.

Bb

backpack

bat

bug

A
B
C
D
E
F
G
H
I
J
K
L
M
N
O
P
Q
R
S
T
U
V
W
X
Y
Z

because

bird

blue

both

buy

blanket

Bb

 bat

 beans

 bug

Bb

backpack

beans

bug

Cc

Last night Corey saw a **camel**

Driving a **car** around town.

Celery filled the front seat to the ceiling,

And the back was packed with **clowns**.

Cc

camel

car

celery

can

circle

cold

come

could

cousins

California

Cardboard

Cc

car

celery

clowns

Cc

camel

celery

clowns

Dd

Denise and Darla sat with their **dolls**

And began to **drink** some tea.

You should have seen the **dishes** fly

When they saw my **duck** and me!

14

Dd

dishes

dolls

drink

A
B
C
D
E
F
G
H
I
J
K
L
M
N
O
P
Q
R
S
T
U
V
W
X
Y
Z

did

do

does

down

draw

done

design

digestive system

 Dd

dishes

drink

duck

Dd

dishes   dolls   duck

Ee

All around the **elephant**

The **eagle** chased the beagle.

The elephant felt a bee on her **ear**—

"Eek!" went the eagle!

E e

eagle

ear

elephant

A
B
C
D
E
F
G
H
I
J
K
L
M
N
O
P
Q
R
S
T
U
V
W
X
Y
Z

eat

egg

eight

every

eye

each EliSheva Ellie

Ee

eagle

ear

elephant

Ee

eagle

ear

elephant

Ff

Four hungry **frogs** sat on a log.

Five fat **flies** floated in the sky.

One forgot and **flew** too close—

Four fat flies in the sky.

Ff

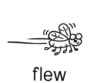
flew   flies

frogs

family   foohy

flower

for

friend

from

fins

Ff

flew

flies

frogs

Ff

 flew

 flies

 frogs

A
B
C
D
E
F
G
H
I
J
K
L
M
N
O
P
Q
R
S
T
U
V
W
X
Y
Z

Gg

 I got a ring with a **gem** like a star,

 A baby **gerbil,** and a fast race car.

 But my favorite birthday **gift** by far

Was what my Grandma sent—a **guitar**!

Gg

gem

gerbil

gift

getting

girl

give

goes

green

grade

 Gg

gerbil

gift

guitar

Gg

gem   gift   guitar

A
B
C
D
E
F
G
H
I
J
K
L
M
N
O
P
Q
R
S
T
U
V
W
X
Y
Z

Hh

Hannah lives at the top of a **hill**.

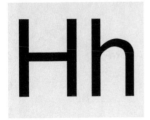

Her **house** is very small.

The mouse and **hen** are perfect pets,

But the **horse** is just too tall.

Hh

hen

hill

house

hand

has

have

here

how

Hollywood

Hh

hen

horse

house

Hh

hen   hill   horse

Ii

Ike moved away to an **island**

Made of **ice** and snow.

He lived in a big chilly **igloo**

With a whiny **iguana** named Moe.

Ii

ice

igloo

island

A B C D E F G H **I** J K L M N O P Q R S T U V W X Y Z

idea

I'm = I + am

inch

into

it's = it + is

I've

Ii

ice

igloo

iguana

I i

igloo

iguana

island

Jj

Jake, you can **juggle** juice in a **jug,**

You can juggle jam in a **jar,**

You can even juggle and tell a joke,

But you just can't juggle a **jaguar.**

Jj

 jar

 jug

 juggle

jaw

jelly

jet

joy

jump

Jj

jaguar   jar   jug

Jj

jaguar

jar

juggle

Kk

Once upon a time there lived a **king**

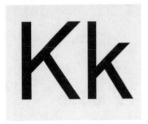

Who met a pretty **kangaroo**.

On his cheek she gave him a **kiss**.

Now he's a kangaroo, too.

Kk

kangaroo

king

kiss

keep

kind

kite

kitten

know

Kindergardeners

Krantz

Kk

 kangaroo

 king

 kiss

Kk

kangaroo

king

kiss

A
B
C
D
E
F
G
H
I
J
K
L
M
N
O
P
Q
R
S
T
U
V
W
X
Y
Z

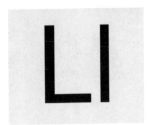

I open up my **lunchbox**

To **look** for food to trade—

She can have my **liver** sandwich,

But she can't have my **lemonade**!

Ll

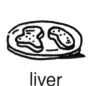
liver

look

lunchbox

later

let's = let + 's

letter

light

love

lemonade

liver

look

Ll

lemonade

liver

lunchbox

A
B
C
D
E
F
G
H
I
J
K
L
M
N
O
P
Q
R
S
T
U
V
W
X
Y
Z

49

Mm

Up the street marched a mighty **moose**

Who found a **mirror** in my house.

He whipped out a **mask** and said to me,

"This moose is now a **mouse**!"

Mm

mask

mirror

moose

many   Mexican

milk

morning

mountain

move

middle

museum

Mm

 mask

 mirror

 mouse

Mm

mask

moose

mouse

Nn

Nathan bought a **needle,**

Some string, and some nice **noodles**.

He worked all **night** to make new collars

9

For three of his **nine** poodles.

Nn

needle

night

noodles

need

noise

noon

not

now

Nn

night

nine

noodles

Nn

needle night nine

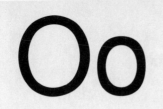

Oo

All over the **ocean** the otter sailed,

An ox and an **ostrich** for crew,

With nothing to eat but old **oatmeal**

And a pot of cold **olive** stew.

Oo

 oatmeal ocean

 ostrich

old

once

one

orange

our

  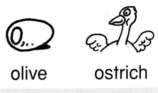

oatmeal olive ostrich

Oo

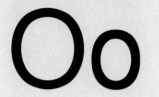

oatmeal

ocean

olive

Pp

The happy **puppy** wagged her tail,

And tipped over the painter's **pail**.

She ran right through the purple **paint,**

And left a **paw**-print trail!

Pp

 pail   paint   puppy

picture

plant

please

pretty

pull

pale

potato

pueblo

Pp

pail

paint

paw

Pp

paint

paw

puppy

A
B
C
D
E
F
G
H
I
J
K
L
M
N
O
P
Q
R
S
T
U
V
W
X
Y
Z

Qq

I need to ask you a **question**.

Which gift is best for a **queen**—

A squeaking squirrel, a quiet **quail,**

Or a **quilt** of gold and green?

Qq

 quail

 queen

 question

quack

quick

quit

Qq

 quail

 queen

 quilt

quail

question

quilt

Rr

Last night I floated down a **river**

On a **raft** by the light of the moon

And read a story about a **rocket**

To a rabbit and a **raccoon**.

Rr

 raft

 river

 rocket

A
B
C
D
E
F
G
H
I
J
K
L
M
N
O
P
Q
R
S
T
U
V
W
X
Y
Z

race

rain

real

right

round

Rr

raccoon

raft

rocket

Rr

raccoon

river

rocket

A
B
C
D
E
F
G
H
I
J
K
L
M
N
O
P
Q
R
S
T
U
V
W
X
Y
Z

Ss

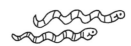

See those slick and slimy **snakes**

Swim slowly out of the sea?

See them slide right over the **sand**—

And **stop** right by my knee?

Ss

 sand
 snakes
 swim

said
suspicious

saw

sleep

some

soon

Sealey's

second

substitate

A B C D E F G H I J K L M N O P Q R **S** T U V W X Y Z

Ss

 sand   stop   swim

Ss

sand

snakes

stop

Snuc

Tt

Turtle bought the **tickets**.

Tiger packed the trunks.

Then they took a short **train** trip

To see **two** lonely skunks.

Tt

tickets

tiger

train

take   *twirled*

tell

their

three 3

too

tyrannasorous

A
B
C
D
E
F
G
H
I
J
K
L
M
N
O
P
Q
R
S
T
U
V
W
X
Y
Z

Tt

tiger

train

two

Tt

tickets

train

two

Uu

My uncle wears a **uniform**.

His name is Hubert James.

His arm flies **up,** and "Out!" he shouts.

He's an **umpire** for baseball games.

Uu

umpire

uniform

up

under

unhappy ☹

until

upon

use

usually

Uu

umpire   uniform   up

Uu

umpire

uniform

up

 Vv

When Valerie drives her fancy **van,**

She wants to look her best.

She wears a hat with a silver **veil**

That matches the **vines** on her **vest**.

Vv

van

veil

vest

vegetable

vet

village

visit

voice

Vv

veil

vest

vines

Vv

van

vest

vines

A
B
C
D
E
F
G
H
I
J
K
L
M
N
O
P
Q
R
S
T
U
V
W
X
Y
Z

Ww

A whale and a **walrus** got a **wagon**

And went out to find a meal.

They found a place with **waffles**

And a **waiter** that was a seal.

Ww

waffles

wagon

walrus

was

watch

where

with

write

waffles   wagon   waiter

Ww

waffles

waiter

walrus

A
B
C
D
E
F
G
H
I
J
K
L
M
N
O
P
Q
R
S
T
U
V
W
X
Y
Z

Xx

"My tummy aches," said the **fox**.

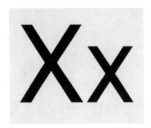

"Let's take an **x-ray,**" said the ox.

"Hmm," the ox said. "Tell me, fox,

Why did you eat **six boxes** of rocks?"

Xx

fox

six

x-ray

xylophone

Xx

boxes

six

x-ray

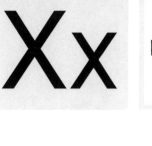

boxes

fox

six

Yy

Yesterday I saw a **yak** in your **yard**.

I heard her **yell** "Yahoo!"

Look! Today she's come back,

And she's brought a **yo-yo** for you!

Yy

yak

yard

yell

year

yellow

yes

you'll = you + will

young

Y y

yard

yell

yo-yo

Yy

yak   yell   yo-yo

Zz

Zack is a **zebra** in our school play,

But his costume won't stay **zipped**.

Even a **zigzag** stitch won't make it stay,

0

So we have **zero** zebras on stage today.

Zz

zebra

‎W‎W

zigzag

zipped

zipper

zoo

zoom

Zz

0
zero

ᴡᴡᴠ
zigzag

zipped

Zz

zebra

zero

zigzag

Social Studies Words

city _____ _____

desert _____ _____

flag ⚑ _____ _____

home _____ _____

law _____ _____

_____ _____

_____ _____

Science Words

cell

energy

gas

mixture

soil

Math Words

add _____   _____

least _____   _____

measure _____   _____

pattern _____   _____

square ☐ _____   _____

_____   _____

_____   _____

_____   _____

Reading and Language Words

clue

describe

idea

past

stories

Art and Music Words

easel _____ _____

paintbrush _____ _____

sketch _____ _____

violin _____ _____

voice _____ _____

_____ _____

_____ _____

_____ _____

Words Often Misspelled

always	caught	funny
about	cheese	get
after	children	girl
again	come	going
and	could	good
another	dad	got
are	didn't	great
around	different	happily
aunt	dinosaur	have
babies	don't	heard
baseball	down	her
beautiful	end	him
because	every	home
before	everybody	house
believe	everything	hurt
bird	family	I'm
birthday	favorite	into
brother	first	is
brought	for	it's
but	found	knew
came	friend	know

like	said	through
little	saw	to
love	scared	too
made	school	took
mom	second	tried
much	sister	two
my	some	upon
next	something	very
nice	sometimes	want
night	special	wanted
of	started	was
once	swimming	watch
one	teacher	went
other	thank	were
our	that	what
out	the	when
outside	their	where
part	them	whole
party	then	will
people	there	witch
play	they	with
presents	they're	world
pretty	think	would
really	thought	yours